Original title:
Habit Formation

Copyright © 2024 Creative Arts Management OÜ
All rights reserved.

Author: Clement Portlander
ISBN HARDBACK: 978-9916-88-338-9
ISBN PAPERBACK: 978-9916-88-339-6

A Journey of a Thousand Steps

Each step I take, a path unfolds,
Through valleys low and mountains bold.
With dreams in heart and hope in hand,
I wander through this wondrous land.

The sun will rise and light my way,
While shadows dance where children play.
With every choice, new stories weave,
And in each moment, I believe.

The winds will whisper tales of old,
Of brave hearts forged in trials cold.
I gather strength from those who've passed,
Their echoes linger, deep and vast.

As twilight falls, the stars alight,
A sign of courage through the night.
So onward I will move with grace,
For every step, my dreams embrace.

The Breath of Repetition

In the cycle of day, we wake and we sleep,
Rhythms repeat like a promise we keep.
Footsteps in patterns, the same paths we tread,
Yet beneath the surface, our spirits are fed.

Whispers of love linger on in the air,
Moments of laughter, the bonds that we share.
In echoes of youth, we find our sweet grace,
The breath of repetition, time's warm embrace.

Choreography of Change

Dancing through seasons, we shift and we sway,
Nature unfolds, guiding us on our way.
Each step a story, each twirl a new chance,
Embrace the uncertainty, join the great dance.

Leaves turn to gold, then scatter like dust,
Transformations whisper, in change we must trust.
With every movement, the world rearranges,
In the choreography of constant changes.

Tesseract of Time

Time folds and stretches like fabric unseen,
Moments converge where the future has been.
Past and present entwined in their flight,
A tesseract gleaming in the folds of the night.

Memories layer like pages in a book,
Each one a doorway, beckoning a look.
In infinity's dance, we glimpse what's to come,
The echoes of seconds, a timeless hum.

The Flow of Familiarity

In the stream of routine, comfort abounds,
Familiar faces, soft laughter resounds.
A sanctuary built of shared little things,
The flow of familiarity warmly clings.

Through tides of our days, we anchor and sway,
In habits of love, we find our own way.
Though waves may crash hard, we stand strong and true,
The flow of familiarity, me and you.

The Gentle Push of Tomorrow

A dawn breaks soft and bright,
Whispers of dreams take flight.
Hope floats on the morning air,
Tomorrow waits, beyond despair.

Each step forward, small yet bold,
Stories of courage yet untold.
In silence, promises are spun,
The future calls, a race begun.

Eyes on horizons, hearts aglow,
In shared visions, together we grow.
With every heartbeat, we ignite,
The gentle push towards the light.

Strokes of Determination

With each brushstroke, dreams unfold,
Colors of courage, tales of old.
On canvas, passion dances free,
In every hue, the heart can see.

Lines that tremble, yet still remain,
In pursuit of joy, we embrace the pain.
With grit and grace, our spirits fly,
Every heartbeat, a steadfast sigh.

Vision shapes the path we tread,
Through stormy nights, our dreams are fed.
With strokes of fire, we redefine,
A masterpiece forged through love and time.

Crafting Continuity

In every thread, a story we weave,
Moments stitched, as we believe.
Together, hands create the flow,
Binding dreams through highs and lows.

Footprints marked on paths we share,
Echoes of laughter fill the air.
With patience, we nurture and sow,
The roots of life in gentle glow.

Connections formed in twilight's grace,
A tapestry of time and space.
Holding close what's true and dear,
Crafting continuity year by year.

Unwritten Scripts of Life

Pages blank, yet stories loom,
In silence, dreams begin to bloom.
With every breath, a tale takes flight,
Unwritten scripts dance in the night.

Whispers echo of paths not taken,
In chance encounters, hearts awaken.
Every moment, a chance to write,
Filling pages with pure delight.

So let us pen what we can see,
With ink of hope, we set it free.
Embracing all, both dark and bright,
Unwritten scripts, our guiding light.

Echoes of Dawn

Soft whispers greet the dawn,
With colors bold and bright.
The sun begins to yawn,
Chasing away the night.

Birds sing their sweet refrain,
In harmony they soar.
Nature stirs from its chain,
Welcoming day once more.

Footsteps on the dew-kissed grass,
A moment's peace in time.
Each second comes to pass,
In nature's perfect rhyme.

Light dances on the stream,
Reflecting every hue.
So vivid is the dream,
As dawn breaks fresh and new.

Chains of Consistency

Life moves in steady waves,
A rhythm that we know.
Each action forms the graves,
Where dreams both ebb and flow.

Moments stacked in a row,
A pattern carved in stone.
In cycles high and low,
We find we're not alone.

Routines that bind and hold,
Through seasons' fleeting grace.
Each story gently told,
Finds strength in every place.

Yet freedom calls our name,
To break the mold we've made.
In stillness, we reclaim,
The spark that will not fade.

The Rhythm of Routine

Morning light breaks anew,
Awakening the day.
In rhythm, life feels true,
As moments softly sway.

Cups of coffee steam and rise,
Steps on familiar paths.
The comfort in the ties,
That lead to our own laughs.

Days loop like a gentle song,
The dance of give and take.
Though some may feel it's wrong,
In time, our hearts won't break.

Embrace each small delight,
In laughter, tears, or sighs.
The rhythm feels so right,
Reflecting in our eyes.

Threads of the Everyday

Woven in mundane threads,
Life's tapestry unfolds.
A fabric of our heads,
With stories yet untold.

Strands of joy and of strife,
In colors bright and dim.
Each moment shapes our life,
And binds us limb to limb.

Glimmers of love do shine,
In chores and tasks we do.
The simple acts align,
Creating something true.

So cherish every thread,
In every twist and turn.
For in these paths we've tread,
Is where our hearts will learn.

The Art of Becoming You

In the mirror, you find the spark,
A journey begins, light in the dark.
Each choice a brushstroke, making it clear,
A masterpiece formed, year by year.

Unfolding layers, stories untold,
Molding the shape of a heart so bold.
Through trials and laughter, color your view,
Embrace every moment, it's all part of you.

In the rhythm of life, dance to your tune,
Under the sun or the light of the moon.
With every heartbeat, grace will ensue,
This beautiful art is the becoming of you.

Landscapes of the Known

Mountains rise in the morning mist,
Paths tell stories that no one can twist.
Fields of gold where the wild winds blow,
A canvas of time, landscapes we know.

Rivers cascade, carving their song,
In every echo, we feel we belong.
Under the vast sky, we find our way,
In nature's embrace, day after day.

Each tree a witness, every stone a friend,
Whispers of wisdom in the branches wend.
Together we wander, together we roam,
In the landscapes of known, we find our home.

Whispers of Repetition

In the silence, soft echoes ring,
A dance of shadows, a familiar spring.
Repetitions weave through the fabric of time,
Each note a reminder, each heartbeat a rhyme.

Cycles of seasons, the sun and the rain,
Lessons revisited, joy wrapped in pain.
In every heartbeat, a story retold,
Whispers of repetition, treasures unfold.

Patterns emerge in the tapestry of days,
In the mundane, magic finds ways.
We learn through the echoes, the gentle embrace,
Whispers of repetition, life's sacred space.

The Seeds We Sow

Tiny grains nestled in the earth,
Holding dreams of potential and worth.
With faith and patience, we tend to the ground,
In the silence of growth, life's magic is found.

Water with hope, nurture with care,
In the garden of life, love is laid bare.
Each seed a promise, each sprout a smile,
Together we flourish, traversing each mile.

Under the sun, we blossom and grow,
The fruits of our labor, the joy that we sow.
In the circle of seasons, our legacy glows,
With each gentle whisper, the seeds that we sow.

The Pulse of Commitment

In whispers soft, a promise flows,
Through trials faced, the heart still grows.
With every beat, a steadfast vow,
In shadows deep, we find our now.

Like rivers bend but never break,
In storms we stand, our ground we stake.
With hands entwined, we brave the night,
The pulse of love, a guiding light.

Moments that Shape

In fleeting glances, time stands still,
A laughter shared, a dream fulfilled.
Each breath we take, a story told,
In simple acts, a heart of gold.

The sun setting on a quiet place,
A gentle smile, a warm embrace.
In every pause, the world aligns,
Moments that shape the heart's designs.

Vignettes of the Everyday

The morning light through window streams,
A coffee cup, the day begins.
In routine walks, we find the grace,
Of life unfolding at its pace.

The chatter of the bustling street,
A child at play, a heart's sweet beat.
In small details, the joy arrives,
Vignettes of life where wonder thrives.

The Sonic Wave of Routine

The clock ticks on, the rhythm plays,
In every task, the heart obeys.
A pulse of sounds, a daily tune,
We dance in time beneath the moon.

With steps aligned, we move in sync,
In simple acts, we find the link.
Through waves of sound, our lives entwine,
Routine's embrace, endlessly divine.

Seeds of Routine

Dawn awakes with tender light,
Seeds of habit take their flight.
Morning coffee, warm embrace,
In this cycle, find my place.

Steps are measured, day anew,
Quiet moments, just a few.
Each small action, roots take hold,
Growing stories, yet untold.

Through the rhythm, life will sway,
In the mundane, dreams at play.
Time a friend, or foe at times,
Yet in patterns, life still climbs.

The Echo of Repetition

Whispers linger in the air,
Echoes soft, without a care.
Days resound in mirrored ways,
Familiar paths through all our days.

In the silence, rhythms blend,
Repetition, a faithful friend.
Every heartbeat, every breath,
Life's reflections, dance with death.

Cyclical, the world will spin,
In each loop, we find within.
In the steady, strength is born,
From each dusk comes every dawn.

Tides of Consistency

Waves of time roll in and out,
Consistent paths, without a doubt.
Every ebb and every flow,
Life's foundation, steady grow.

Beneath the surface, currents churn,
In the quiet, lessons learn.
Change may come, yet still we stand,
In the rhythm, life's command.

Footprints traced on sandy shores,
Marking moments, opening doors.
Tides of time will shape our way,
In the cycle, night and day.

Patterns in the Twilight

Softly fades the light of day,
Twilight brings shadows at play.
Shapes and forms, the world at rest,
In the quiet, we are blessed.

Mingling tones of dark and bright,
Patterns dance in evening light.
With each whisper, stories weave,
In the silence, hearts believe.

Time suspended, moments freeze,
In the twilight, thoughts find ease.
Every breath a tapestry,
In the dusk, we yearn to be.

The Mechanism of Change

In shadows deep, we seek the light,
A whisper calls, igniting flight.
The gears of fate begin to turn,
In every heart, a fire will burn.

With courage found, we shape our fate,
A journey starts, we cannot wait.
From doubt to strength, we break the mold,
In every story, change unfolds.

Through valleys low and mountains high,
We rise again, we touch the sky.
Each step we take, a chance to grow,
In every heart, the seeds we sow.

So let us dance, embrace the risk,
For change is life, a vibrant whisk.
In every ending, a new embrace,
The mechanism, a sacred space.

A Chorus of Choices

In quiet moments, paths appear,
A symphony, both far and near.
Each note a choice, a step we take,
In every heart, a chance to wake.

With open minds, we share the song,
The chorus swells, we all belong.
In unity, our voices blend,
Together strong, our spirits mend.

Through trials faced, we rise anew,
The choices made, both false and true.
Each turn of fate, a lesson learned,
In every heart, a fire burned.

So let us sing, and let us dance,
Embrace the fate, the fleeting chance.
In harmony, we find our way,
A chorus bright, come what may.

The Balance of Practice

In every step, we find the flow,
The rhythm guides, a gentle glow.
With practice found in night and day,
We find our strength, come what may.

Each stumble met, a lesson clear,
In perseverance, we conquer fear.
The balance struck between the strife,
A dance that weaves the thread of life.

With patience sown, we start to bloom,
In quiet hours, we chase the gloom.
The art of skill, a steady hand,
In every heartbeat, we make our stand.

So let us strive, with purpose grand,
A journey shared, together we stand.
In practice true, we shape and grow,
The balance found, in ebb and flow.

Silhouettes of Determination

In twilight's hue, we stand as one,
Silhouettes cast, our battles won.
With fierce resolve, we chase the dream,
In shadows deep, we find the beam.

Each figure strong, each heart aglow,
Through darkest nights, we learn to grow.
We carve our paths, with grit and grace,
In every challenge, we find our place.

With voices raised, we break the chains,
In unity, we bear the pains.
Determined souls, relentless fight,
In every struggle, we claim our light.

So let us rise, our spirits bold,
In silhouettes, our stories told.
With every step, we pave the way,
Determination lights the day.

The Tightrope of Tenacity

Each step is fraught with fear,
Yet I walk with a steady heart.
Balancing dreams and doubt,
My will is the work of art.

The winds may howl and sway,
But my focus sharpens tight.
With each breath, I dare to stay,
On this line of hopeful light.

Underneath the chaos roars,
A strength not often seen.
Resilience opens doors,
As I cling to what has been.

The journey's fraught with strain,
Yet I shall not retreat.
For the courage in my veins,
Guides my feet on this thin sheet.

Foundations Beneath the Surface

Beneath the sand, the roots run deep,
In silence, they bend and grow.
Hidden strength, a secret keep,
Whispers of what we don't know.

The world above may shift and sway,
Yet beneath lies solid ground.
With every storm, the trees stay,
In unity, they are bound.

Though many times we'll face the storm,
With patience, we stand tall.
Our bonds reshape, break the norm,
Foundations will not fall.

The unseen threads connect us all,
In shadows, we find light.
Together, we will never crawl,
For our roots hold us tight.

The Weaving of Will

Threads of fate intertwine,
Patterns emerge with grace.
Each decision, a single line,
Crafting a delicate space.

With hands that tremble, yet steady,
I stitch together dreams.
A fabric of hope, ever ready,
Unraveling at the seams.

Colors of passion, shades of fear,
Mixing in a vibrant blend.
The heartbeat of purpose is clear,
In every twist, we mend.

Through trials, we learn to bind,
Creating a tapestry bright.
In the fabric of life, we're intertwined,
Our stories woven tight.

Meanings Carved in Time

Every moment leaves its mark,
Whispers of what's gone by.
Carved in stone, yet ever stark,
Echoing the future's cry.

The hands of time move slow,
Yet lessons shape our way.
In shadows of long ago,
We find the light of day.

With memories etched in sand,
Life shifts with every tide.
Finding peace within this land,
Where past and present glide.

Meanings shift, evolve, and grow,
As we tread this winding path.
In every high and mighty blow,
We forge our own aftermath.

Rituals of the Dawn

Whispers greet the breaking light,
Birds ascend in graceful flight,
Morning dew upon the grass,
Nature stirs as night must pass.

Chants of life fill the cool air,
Awakening with purpose rare,
Each petal opens to embrace,
The sun's warm kiss, a sweet grace.

Time unfolds in golden hues,
Painting skies with vibrant views,
Shadows stretch then fade away,
In the dawn's soft, tender play.

Every heart begins to beat,
In this ritual, pure and sweet,
A promise born with each new day,
As night's soft whispers fade away.

Tapestry of Intent

Threads of thought weave through the mind,
Colors mingle, intertwined,
Each intention, a vibrant thread,
In the fabric where dreams are spread.

A tapestry, rich and complete,
Patterns grow with every heartbeat,
Woven stories, hopes and fears,
Stitched together through the years.

Every knot holds a sacred place,
In this quilt of time and space,
With every choice, the pattern shifts,
Creating life's most precious gifts.

In the loom of night and day,
We craft the dreams that guide our way,
A mosaic of paths we take,
In the tapestry we awake.

Architecture of the Ordinary

Bricks and beams, a silent song,
In structures where we all belong,
Every corner tells a tale,
In quiet moments, life prevails.

Windows open to the past,
Frames of life, memories cast,
Each room holds a world within,
A sanctuary where we begin.

Streets are veins, pulsing with life,
Echoes of joy, sorrow, and strife,
As sunlight dances on the walls,
In this haven, wonder calls.

In the ordinary, magic gleams,
Found in whispers, hopes, and dreams,
Architecture shaped by love and care,
In every detail, stories share.

The Cycle of Becoming

Seeds are sown beneath the earth,
Whispers of future, dreams of birth,
In silence, life begins to stir,
As worlds awaken, they confer.

Roots dig deep, seeking the light,
In darkness growing, taking flight,
Branches reach for skies so wide,
In the dance of life's great tide.

Each moment shapes what's yet to be,
In cycles spun eternally,
Time unfolding, ever true,
In this journey, we renew.

From dusk to dawn, the flow persists,
In becoming, we find our bliss,
As nature whispers soft and clear,
Embrace the cycle, hold it dear.

Navigating the Unworn Path

In shadows deep, the journey lies,
Where few have tread, beneath green skies.
With every step, the silence sings,
A call to chase what freedom brings.

The forest speaks in rustling leaves,
Of hidden truths that one believes.
The stars above, a guiding light,
Through tangled woods, into the night.

With courage forged, I meet the dawn,
Each fear released, each worry gone.
The path unfolds, a tale untold,
In nature's arms, I am consoled.

At every turn, new wonders show,
The heart expands, its warmth aglow.
Though unworn paths may seem unclear,
The spirit knows, there is no fear.

The Map of Familiarity

In streets well-worn, I find my way,
Each corner holds a memory's play.
The shops and homes that line the road,
In their embrace, my heart's abode.

Worn doors creak with a story told,
Of laughter shared and comforts old.
The sunset paints the skyline bright,
In this familiar, I feel right.

Beneath the stars, my roots run deep,
Here in this place, my soul can sleep.
The map I hold is drawn with care,
With every step, I've left a share.

Yet even here, some paths are new,
A twist, a turn, a shift in view.
Within these streets, I still can roam,
For every step, I find my home.

Whispers in the Wind

The breeze carries secrets of the past,
Through fields and trees, its shadows cast.
With every rustle, a tale begins,
Of timeless echoes, where silence spins.

The mountains listen, their peaks held high,
Each whisper flows, like clouds in the sky.
Nature's voice, gentle yet bold,
In the whispering winds, stories unfold.

A dance of leaves, the branches sway,
In every gust, a choice to stay.
For spirits roam in the airy stretch,
Inviting hearts, their dreams to fetch.

So when you hear the softest call,
Take time to pause, heed the thrall.
In whispers found, the truth unfurled,
Life's gentle breath, a wondrous world.

Stone and Habit

We build our lives on stones so clear,
With every habit, we draw near.
From simple paths to winding trails,
In steady rhythms, our heart prevails.

The weight of hours, both light and dense,
Crafts the terrain, our thoughts immense.
Each stone we place, a choice made firm,
In life's great dance, it's habit's term.

Yet change demands a chisel's art,
To carve new ways, to play our part.
With patience, we can shape the stone,
And find new habits we can own.

So let us tread with wisdom's gaze,
Through roughened paths and gentle ways.
In every stone, a story kept,
In habits formed, our dreams adept.

Anchors and Avenues

Beneath the sky so wide and bright,
Anchors hold in stormy night.
Avenues stretch, both near and far,
Guiding dreams like a shining star.

Waves may crash, and winds may howl,
Yet steadfast hearts remain a prowl.
In every port, a tale to weave,
Reflections of what we believe.

The path is long, but solace found,
In every tie that's tightly wound.
Anchors deep in friendship's tide,
Avenues where love can bide.

Through every trial, our roots stay strong,
Together we sing our lasting song.
With every step, our spirits soar,
Anchors and avenues to explore.

Circles of Commitment

In sacred space, our vows align,
Circles drawn, forever entwined.
Hand in hand, we face the day,
With whispered truths that light the way.

Every promise, a thread of gold,
In the tapestry of stories told.
Circles turning, seasons change,
Yet our love, it stays the same.

Through trials faced and joys embraced,
In circles of commitment, we are graced.
With open hearts, we build our home,
No more shall we ever roam.

Together we spin a life so bright,
In the circle's warmth, we find our light.
With every breath, our bond renewed,
In circles of love, we are imbued.

The Path Less Worn

Through shadows deep and thickets tight,
The path less worn comes into sight.
With every step, a choice we make,
To forge ahead, embrace the break.

Unfolding leaves in golden hue,
Awakened dreams, a world so new.
The road may twist, the journey long,
Yet in our hearts, we find our song.

With courage bright, we shed all fear,
On the path less worn, we persevere.
In solitude, our spirits rise,
The unknown whispers, a sweet surprise.

Together we tread on untried ground,
In the silence, our joys abound.
With every step, a story spun,
On the path less worn, we are one.

Vows of the Mundane

In morning light, we greet the day,
With humble vows, we find our way.
Amidst the chores and daily grind,
Love's quiet strength is what we find.

Each cup of coffee shared anew,
In laughter soft, our spirits grew.
The mundane moments, often ignored,
Hold promises that can't be stored.

In silence shared, in glances brief,
We pledge our hearts, beyond belief.
Through every task and every plight,
We stitch our lives, both day and night.

Through dust and time, our love remains,
In vows of mundane, joy sustains.
In simple threads, our tapestry,
A life entwined, just you and me.

Morning Rituals

The sun peeks through the trees,
Soft whispers of the dawn.
A cup of tea in hand,
A new day to be drawn.

Gentle breezes in the air,
Birds sing their sweet refrain.
Moments pause to savor,
As nature calls again.

Footsteps on the gravel path,
The world begins to wake.
Each breath a fresh embrace,
With every move we make.

The morning light glimmers bright,
Hope dances in the glow.
In simple, quiet rituals,
Life's beauty starts to show.

Stones in a Stream

Smooth and cool beneath my touch,
Beneath the rush of flow.
Each stone holds a story dear,
Of time that moves so slow.

Water carves their edges fine,
In whispers and in sighs.
They nestle deep in currents clear,
Beneath the open skies.

Light dances on their surfaces,
Time trails past in dreams.
They shift with every ripple's grace,
In nature's flowing schemes.

Yet still they stand, unmoved by time,
A testament to change.
In streams of life, they anchor deep,
In patterns here arranged.

Tides of Change

Waves crash upon the shore,
A melody of the sea.
With every ebb and flow,
They whisper change to me.

Moments rise like ocean tides,
Then slip away like sand.
I watch the world transform,
As life shifts in my hand.

Colors blend in sunset skies,
Past the horizon's dream.
In twilight's soft embrace,
All is not as it seems.

Yet in the heart of change,
Lies beauty yet to find.
Each wave a fleeting gift,
In the ocean of the mind.

The Constant Treader

With every step I wander forth,
On paths both new and worn.
The earth beneath my feet,
Where countless souls were born.

Through forest trails and city streets,
I trace a journey wide.
The rhythm of a traveler,
In nature's arms I bide.

Each moment holds a purpose clear,
With lessons that they share.
The constant treader moves ahead,
With courage I will dare.

In every footfall, history,
In every turn, a chance.
Life's tapestry unfolds;
With every step, I dance.

Shadows of Intent

In the twilight, whispers glide,
Secrets linger, hopes abide.
Shadows dance, intentions clear,
Guiding hearts that we hold dear.

In the depths, where fears reside,
A flicker of light will help us guide.
With every step we take in trust,
We build a path from dreams to dust.

In stillness echoes softly call,
A tapestry of rise and fall.
In shadows cast, our truths unfold,
A story written, brave and bold.

With every heartbeat, feel the sway,
Of choices made along the way.
In longing glances, find the thread,
In shadows of intent, we're led.

The Climb of the Unseen

Upon the ridge, the silent call,
The hidden path awaits us all.
With every step, we search for light,
In shadows deep, our dreams take flight.

The wind whispers secrets untold,
Of wishes whispered, and courage bold.
Fingers clasped on rocks rough and tough,
In this ascent, we've grown enough.

With aching limbs and hearts aglow,
We inch towards heights where few dare go.
Each stumble teaches us to stand,
And mold our fate with steady hand.

At the summit, the world unfolds,
A tapestry of stories told.
From unseen depths, we've found our way,
In the climb's embrace, we learn to sway.

A Symphony of Small Things

In morning light, the dew drops shine,
A symphony of whispers divine.
Each blade of grass, a note so pure,
In nature's choir, we find the cure.

The flutter of a butterfly's wings,
Reminds us of the joy that spring brings.
A child's laughter, a bubbling brook,
In the small things, new worlds we look.

The rustle of leaves in autumn's embrace,
A melody found in time and space.
With every heartbeat, the pulse of earth,
In small things, we find rebirth.

Through the passage of moments we bind,
In simple pleasures, calmness we find.
A symphony, an endless throng,
In the small things, we all belong.

The Weight of Transitions

As seasons shift, the air grows strange,
A subtle shift, a weight, a change.
Leaves fall softly, the sky turns grey,
In each transition, we learn to sway.

The echo of laughter lingers still,
As we embrace the void and fill.
A journey forth through paths unknown,
In every ending, seeds are sown.

Fleeting moments, memories cling,
In silence rests the songs we sing.
With open hearts, we dare to leap,
Into the depths that dreams can keep.

Through twilight dusk, the stars ignite,
Guiding souls, their paths alight.
In transitions, we find our might,
Embracing change, we take flight.

A Journey in Circles

Round and round the path we tread,
Chasing dreams that rarely spread.
Steps that echo in the night,
Facing shadows, seeking light.

Looping back to where we start,
With heavy mind and hopeful heart.
Each turn a lesson learned in time,
Yet still we dance, a rhythm sublime.

Time retreats, yet moments catch,
Binding us in a timeless match.
Every spiral, a story told,
A journey crafted, brave and bold.

In circles we find our way back,
New visions found in old track.
With fresh eyes, the scene we see,
In every loop, there's harmony.

Conversations with Routine

Morning whispers, sun's embrace,
In quiet hours, we find our place.
Familiar rhythms, soft and slow,
In the mundane, seeds of growth.

Coffee brews, the clock ticks near,
Each moment speaks, both loud and clear.
In daily tasks, we weave a thread,
A tapestry where dreams are fed.

Patterns shift, yet comfort stays,
Conversations in familiar ways.
Routine dances, gently guides,
Through life's currents, it abides.

In the mundane, magic hides,
Through simple acts, the soul resides.
We learn to cherish every turn,
In daily rhythms, we discern.

The Mosaic of Daily Choices

Each choice a tile, a moment bright,
In the mosaic, colors ignite.
Fragments of life, arranged with care,
A masterpiece, unique and rare.

Paths diverge at every stop,
Decisions made, we rise or drop.
Glimmers of hope in varied hue,
Every choice an echo true.

We gather pieces, old and new,
With every choice, ourselves we grew.
Embracing flaws, the cracks we mend,
In this mosaic, our lives blend.

Art of living, choice by choice,
In each decision, we find our voice.
With love and courage, we perceive,
In this unique art, we believe.

The Palette of Persistence

Colors blend in thick array,
With strokes of struggle, dawns the day.
Each hue a tale of battles fought,
In persistence, wisdom sought.

Brush in hand, we paint the fight,
On canvas broad, we find our light.
Every failure, a shade refined,
In every setback, strength aligned.

With the palette, we choose to stand,
Crafting dreams with steady hand.
Layers deepen, rich and bold,
In persistence, our story is told.

Through trials faced, we learn to grow,
In every stroke, the passion flows.
A masterpiece of grit and grace,
Our lives a canvas, time's embrace.

Edges of the Ordinary

In corners where shadows dance,
Life whispers softly, a fleeting chance.
Forgotten spaces, a gentle sigh,
Beauty lingers, though we may pass by.

Moments caught in the morning light,
Unseen wonders, a quiet delight.
The fabric of life, woven with thread,
In edges we find the paths we tread.

Familiar faces, a knowing glance,
In the mundane, we find our stance.
A cup of tea, a shared embrace,
In the ordinary, we find our place.

So let us seek in the everyday,
The magic hidden in a simple way.
In the edges, we learn to see,
The beauty of life's small tapestry.

Patterns of Persistence

Through the storms and through the rain,
We rise again, embracing pain.
In the struggles, our spirit sings,
A dance of hope that life still brings.

Each setback a lesson, each fall a stride,
In the heart's resolve, we try to abide.
The threads of strength, tightly spun,
In the patterns of life, we slowly run.

Beneath the surface, resilience grows,
In the quiet moments, our courage shows.
Step by step on the path of grace,
In persistence, we find our place.

With every heartbeat, we push on through,
In the tapestry of life, we weave anew.
For every challenge, there is a way,
In the patterns of persistence, we find our sway.

The Garden of Daily Tasks

In the morning light, the day begins,
With quiet chores and gentle spins.
We tend to life with simple hands,
In each small act, the heart expands.

Sweeping leaves, a rhythmic dance,
In mundane tasks, we find our chance.
Watering dreams, nurturing care,
In daily gardens, love we share.

The scent of bread, the warmth of sun,
In every moment, life's joys run.
Digging deep in the soil so rich,
Finding peace in every stitch.

As seasons change and time unfolds,
In daily tasks, our story holds.
We cultivate joy in fields of green,
In the garden of life, we find the unseen.

Sculpting the Invisible

With every thought, a shape is born,
In the silence, dreams are worn.
Carving moments from fleeting air,
Sculpting shadows, a tender care.

The artist's hand, unseen yet felt,
In whispers of fate, our hearts are knelt.
Chiseling time, each breath a stroke,
In the void, we find the hope.

A vision formed from quiet depths,
In every heartbeat, we take our steps.
Creating worlds that cannot be seen,
In the realm of dreams, we glean.

So let us shape the paths we tread,
With love and courage, we forge ahead.
In the invisible, we find our voice,
Sculpting our lives, a humble choice.

Navigating the Known

In paths of shadow, light will play,
We tread the lines of day by day.
With courage strong, we face the rain,
The map we make, through joy and pain.

Waves of thought like whispers roll,
We search for truths, we seek the whole.
In every choice, a lesson learned,
Through every fall, a fire burned.

The river bends, yet we remain,
In footprints soft, in fleeting grain.
With open hearts, we sail the breeze,
Embrace the struggle, find our ease.

Through winds of change, we'll find our way,
With every dusk, a bright new day.
In known terrains, our spirits soar,
Navigating life, forevermore.

Refrain of the Mundane

In cycles round, the days unfold,
We gather stories, brave and bold.
The morning light, the evening sigh,
Each moment sings, as time slips by.

Routine wraps us in its warm embrace,
In gentle gestures, we find our place.
With every task, a rhythm found,
In mundane beats, our hearts resound.

Yet in the drift of daily grind,
We seek the spark that's undefined.
A fleeting glance, a laugh, a nod,
In silent echoes, life feels odd.

But here within the simple sway,
We cherish all, come what may.
In quiet joys, beneath the sun,
The mundane sings, we'll not outrun.

The Art of Renewal

From ashes cold, new embers glow,
In every end, a chance to grow.
We shed the past like autumn leaves,
In every breath, the spirit weaves.

With open hands, we craft anew,
Each dawn arrives, a canvas true.
Brushstrokes bold, in colors bright,
Reviving dreams, igniting light.

The storms that roar, the quiet streams,
In nature's hand, we find our dreams.
With every cycle, life in flow,
The art of change begins to show.

So take a step, embrace the flow,
In every heart, the seeds we sow.
With hopes aflame, we dance and spin,
In art of renewal, we begin.

Building Bridges to Tomorrow

With every stone, a path is laid,
In hopes and dreams, our fears allayed.
Brick by brick, we rise and build,
In shared resolve, our hearts are filled.

Across the chasm, hands extend,
With laughter bright, and voices blend.
Through trials shared, we find the way,
To brighter futures, come what may.

The sunlight streams on fragile ground,
In unity, our strength is found.
With every stride, we bind the past,
To open doors, our dreams held fast.

Together strong, we'll face the dawn,
In every moment, we press on.
With bridges built, we stand as one,
Towards tomorrow, a new day's sun.

The Architecture of Assurance

In the quiet halls of thought,
Confidence stands tall and strong.
Brick by brick, we build our dreams,
Foundation laid where we belong.

Each pillar bears the weight we hold,
Promises etched in stone so pure.
Windows wide to let hope in,
Each glance a gaze, a heart secured.

Together we construct our fate,
With trust and love, we intertwine.
The roof, a shield from stormy skies,
In this safe space, our spirits shine.

A tapestry of faith unfolds,
Each thread a story, woven tight.
In this architecture, we will thrive,
Assurance guides us through the night.

Caged in Consistency

Within these walls we dwell each day,
Routine wraps tight like a steel cage.
Ticking clocks mark seconds gone,
Comfort found in the mundane stage.

Harmony hums a soothing tune,
Predictable steps lead us along.
Yet in the shadows, whispers creep,
Challenging where we think we belong.

A bird may sing of freedom's call,
Yet fears reside where the heart confines.
In consistency, we find our peace,
But at what cost are we on the lines?

Can we break free from this embrace?
Or shall we dance to the constant beat?
Caged yet safe in a world so small,
Seeking balance, our souls repeat.

Paths Forged in Repetition

Step by step, we walk the line,
Familiar footsteps in the dust.
Circles drawn with every turn,
In the known, we often trust.

Paths like rivers carve their course,
Flowing through the heart and mind.
Each echo of a memory,
A reminder of what we leave behind.

In every stride, we find our way,
The rhythm guides us day by day.
Yet as we travel these old pathways,
Do we lose the chance to sway?

A tapestry of trails we weave,
In repetition, comfort grows.
Yet dreams await beyond the bends,
In the unknown, a spark bestows.

Living the Unremarkable

In simple spaces, lives unfold,
Whispers of the everyday.
Tea leaves settle, stories told,
In the unremarkable, we stay.

Each waking moment blends with time,
In mundane acts, we find our grace.
The beauty of the quiet life,
In each warm smile, in each embrace.

We linger in the golden hour,
As sunlight spills on faded walls.
Finding joy in honest tasks,
In the echoes of familiar calls.

Yet under layers of the usual,
A pulse of dreams resides in still.
In living softly, we discover,
The unremarkable can fulfill.

Ballet of Repetition

In a dance of day and night,
We spin to the same old tune,
Each step a noted plight,
Under the watchful moon.

With every twirl and sway,
Familiar paths we tread,
Lost in the ballet,
Where echoes of dreams are fed.

A rhythm born of trust,
In shadows cast by time,
With whispers turned to dust,
Like whispers turned to rhyme.

Yet through the veils we find,
A spark within the grey,
A new dance intertwined,
In the light of break of day.

Shadows of Custom

In the corners of our minds,
Tradition's whispers cling,
Echoes of what one finds,
In the stories life can bring.

Each gesture, each refrain,
Holds a history untold,
Yet within the mundane,
Life's new chapters unfold.

The dance of norms in place,
A masquerade of thought,
Yet beyond the custom's face,
Lies the freedom sought.

We shape our own design,
With ribbons of the past,
In shadows, we align,
For futures not yet cast.

Weaving the Unseen

Threads of dreams entwined,
In a tapestry of hope,
Patterns yet defined,
In the weaver's gentle scope.

Each stitch a silent prayer,
Invisible to the eye,
Yet carried in the air,
As the moments flutter by.

Colors blend and shift,
In the loom of our design,
Crafting every gift,
With time's delicate line.

Beneath the fabric's glow,
The truth begins to gleam,
A world we long to know,
In the threads of every dream.

Pillars of the Routine

In the dawn of every day,
We rise to face the light,
With pillars firm in a way,
Carved of our shared plight.

Routine whispers softly,
In the patterns we embrace,
A subtle kind of lofty,
That time cannot erase.

With each measured beat,
Stability we crave,
Yet in the heart's retreat,
A pulse too strong to save.

So we dance round and round,
In circles we construct,
While yearning to be found,
In the chaos we conduct.

Sculpting the Self

In silence I carve my stone,
Each chip reveals my core,
With every stroke, I'm not alone,
A journey to explore.

The mirror reflects my quest,
An artist, shadowed light,
With patience, I find the best,
In darkness, I ignite.

Transcending past's heavy mold,
I shape what's true within,
Resilience, brave and bold,
The greater fight I win.

Each flaw becomes a thread,
In fabric of my soul,
From ashes of the dead,
I rise, I am made whole.

Dance of Frequency

In rhythm, hearts entwine,
The pulse of distant stars,
We sway to waves, divine,
In tune with cosmic bars.

A melody unspoken,
In silence, we perceive,
The bonds that once were broken,
In frequencies, believe.

The dance ignites the spark,
In movement, life unfolds,
Two souls in gentle arc,
More vibrant than pure gold.

As echoes fill the air,
We resonate as one,
Embracing every flare,
As shadows turn to sun.

Small Steps to Tomorrow

Each morning brings a chance,
To rise and greet the day,
With hope, I start my dance,
In small steps, I find my way.

They may be quiet moves,
But in their strength, I trust,
In every twist, it proves,
That progress comes from dust.

With courage as my guide,
I tread on paths unknown,
In faith, I will abide,
For seeds of light are sown.

With patience, I will climb,
The peaks of dreams ahead,
Embracing every rhyme,
In moments softly said.

The Alchemy of Practice

In the crucible of time,
I mold the clay of thought,
With repetition, I climb,
To mastery, I'm caught.

Every stroke, a lesson learned,
In fire, my spirit's gained,
With passion ever burned,
From failures, strength obtained.

In twilight's soft embrace,
I grit my teeth, remain,
Through challenges I face,
In joy and even pain.

The gold within the grind,
Emerging crystal clear,
In practice, life aligned,
I gather dreams held dear.

Labyrinth of Choices

In the maze where shadows play,
Paths collide, then drift away.
Each turn whispers in the night,
Hopes and fears in fading light.

Footsteps echo in the hush,
Wanderers in silent rush.
Every choice a thread we weave,
In this web, we learn to grieve.

A fork reveals the heart's desire,
Yet still can quench the brightest fire.
Through twisted halls, the heart can roam,
Seeking solace, yet far from home.

A labyrinth of dreams, entwined,
Where truth and doubt are intertwined.
The journey shapes who we become,
In choices made, new paths will come.

Echoes of Tomorrow

In whispers soft, the future calls,
Through fractured light, the shadow falls.
Each moment breathes a distant sound,
In echoes lost, where hopes are found.

Tomorrow dances on the edge,
With dreams wrapped tight in a solemn pledge.
Steps we take on fragile ground,
Lead to places profound and unbound.

Time flows like a river wide,
Carrying wishes we cannot hide.
Each heartbeat holds the weight of chance,
The past and future in a dance.

In twilight's glow, we cast our gaze,
To the horizon, in fleeting phase.
With every dawn, a chance reborn,
In echoes of tomorrow, hope is sworn.

Crafters of Regularity

With steady hands, we shape the day,
In patterns set, we find our way.
Through monotony, we weave our dreams,
A tapestry of silent themes.

Each sunrise paints the canvas bare,
Tasks in line, we seldom spare.
Yet in the mundane, magic swells,
In quiet moments, the heart dwells.

Routine holds a calming hand,
Creating peace in shifting sand.
The pulse of lives in rhythm beat,
In cadence found, we feel complete.

So hold the thread, embrace the flow,
For in the regular, wonders grow.
Crafters of time, we mold and make,
In daily grace, our souls awake.

Colors of the Mundane

In hues of gray, the world unfolds,
Daily stories, quietly told.
Brushstrokes of life, simple and clear,
Find beauty in all, far and near.

The rust on gates, the cracks in walls,
Each whisper echoes, the heart enthralls.
From coffee stains to worn-out shoes,
In every shade, a life we choose.

Through bustling streets, the colors blend,
A tapestry where all extend.
The laughter shared, the tears that flow,
In colors bright, our spirits grow.

So revel in the earth-toned skies,
In every glance, the true surprise.
For in the mundane, treasures wait,
In subtleties, we find our fate.

Unseen Forces of Change

Whispers in the quiet night,
Softly shifting all in sight.
Gentle winds that bend the trees,
Carrying dreams with subtle ease.

Rippling streams that tell a tale,
Of hidden paths and unseen trails.
In shadows dance the sparks of light,
Guiding souls to take their flight.

Echoes linger, hearts will learn,
In every corner, tides will turn.
Change will come, at times unknown,
Like seeds that grow from earth alone.

So trust the pull of time's embrace,
For in the darkness lies a grace.
The unseen forces shape our fate,
In every moment, change awaits.

Oaths on Repeat

Promises woven, threads of gold,
Words exchanged in tales retold.
Hearts beat steady, firm and true,
In every vow, a love anew.

In quiet mornings, oaths arise,
In whispered dreams, beneath the skies.
Guardians of each sacred pledge,
Together we stand, on every edge.

Through storms we march, united still,
Bound by desires, unyielding will.
Reaffirming what we hold dear,
In every heartbeat, love draws near.

While time may twist, the words remain,
A melody that soothes our pain.
In endless echoes, love's retreat,
We find our strength in oaths complete.

The Craft of Daily Design

Each morning brings a brand new chance,
To sketch a life, to dream, to dance.
With every choice, the canvas shows,
The beauty in what daily grows.

Brush strokes of laughter, hues of care,
In simple moments, love lays bare.
Colors blend in joyful play,
As we craft our lives each day.

Thoughts like seeds in fertile ground,
In every act, new dreams are found.
The art of living, bold and bright,
Transcends the dark, ignites the light.

With hearts as tools, we shape our way,
In life's design, we find our sway.
A masterpiece in time aligned,
Crafted with love, beautifully twined.

Seasons of Resilience

Winter's chill may test the soul,
Yet in the frost, we find our whole.
Each season shifts, the cycle spins,
In every end, a new life begins.

Spring brings blooms from dormant seeds,
In vibrant hues, the heart proceeds.
Through trials faced with quiet grace,
Resilience shines on every face.

Summer's warmth, the sunlit glow,
Nurtures life and lets love grow.
In laughter shared under blue skies,
Strength is born as spirit flies.

Autumn whispers, time's embrace,
Leaves that dance, a slow-paced race.
We gather strength from all that's passed,
For in each season, we hold fast.

The Rhythm of Daily Steps

In morning light, we rise anew,
With every breath, we start our tune.
Feet on the path, a steady beat,
Each step a note, a life replete.

Through winding streets, we find our way,
The world unfolds, both bright and gray.
In laughter shared and silence held,
Our journey sings, as dreams compel.

With simple acts, our lives entwine,
In every gesture, love can shine.
The rhythm flows, both soft and strong,
A melody where we belong.

As night descends, we pause to rest,
Reflecting on the day's behest.
In quiet moments, wisdom grows,
Each step a thread, life's tapestry shows.

Threads of the Everyday

Morning coffee, warm embrace,
A woven routine, a sacred space.
Chores and laughter side by side,
In simple joys, our hearts abide.

Children's smiles, a fleeting glance,
Moments captured in life's dance.
Each tiny thread, a story spun,
In everyday seconds, we find the fun.

Evening whispers, light dims low,
The fabric of life, the ebb and flow.
Connections made, both strong and slight,
In threads of love, we find our light.

In the tapestry, we leave our mark,
Every stitch a spark in the dark.
Woven together, rich and vast,
The threads of life, forever cast.

Choreography of the Mind

Thoughts pirouette, in quiet grace,
Dancing lightly in time and space.
Ideas twirl, a vibrant show,
In the theater of the mind, they flow.

Reflections merge and ebb like tides,
Through corridors where wisdom hides.
In the stillness, clarity forms,
A ballet of dreams, where spirit warms.

The rhythm pulses, a heartbeat's call,
In the silence, our dreams enthrall.
With each new thought, our souls take flight,
A choreography of dark and light.

In every moment, an art unfolds,
Canvas vast, with tales untold.
The mind's ballet, both fierce and kind,
Dances forever, unconfined.

Sculpting the Familiar

In gentle hands, we shape our days,
Carving moments in myriad ways.
Familiar paths, yet new and bold,
In sculptor's care, our lives unfold.

Each touch a grace, each breath a mold,
Creating warmth from the mundane cold.
With patience, we refine the stone,
In every crack, a beauty shown.

Routines like clay, we press and knead,
In the art of life, we plant the seed.
Familiar echoes, tender and soft,
In every heartbeat, we lift aloft.

As shadows dance on evening walls,
In our creation, the silence calls.
To sculpt the world, both great and small,
In every moment, we embrace it all.

Threads Woven by Time

In the loom of memory we dwell,
Each thread a story we weave so well.
Time stitches moments with gentle care,
Binding the fabric of hopes laid bare.

Whispers of ages in every strand,
Lifetimes captured in a delicate hand.
Colors of laughter, shades of pain,
Woven together through sunshine and rain.

Each knot a lesson, each weave a sigh,
Patterns reflecting the days gone by.
With every loop, a heartbeat traced,
In the tapestry of life, cherished and spaced.

As the wheel of time continues to turn,
New threads emerge, new stories to learn.
In this intricate design, we find our grace,
Threads woven by time, our sacred place.

The Canvas of Could Be

A blank canvas stretched, wide and free,
Whispers of dreams paint what could be.
Strokes of passion in colors bright,
Imagining futures, igniting light.

In hues of hope, possibilities swirl,
Each brushstroke dances, each thought unfurls.
Visions emerge from the depths of the mind,
A masterpiece waiting, uniquely designed.

Splatters of laughter, splashes of tears,
The canvas absorbs our joys and fears.
With every creation, a story unfolds,
The art of our lives, in colors bold.

So let us create, let us explore,
On the canvas of could be, forever more.
Each day a new hue, each moment a chance,
To live in the beauty of this vibrant dance.

Seeds of Intent

In the garden of thoughts, seeds we sow,
With intention and purpose, we watch them grow.
Nurturing dreams in the fertile ground,
Roots of resolve spreading all around.

Each idea a sprout, reaching for light,
Watered with passion, they flourish bright.
Planted with care, we tend to our goals,
Harvesting wisdom that nourishes souls.

As seasons change, we prune and we shape,
Guiding our visions, our own escape.
The fruits of our effort, sweet to taste,
As we gather moments, never to waste.

With heart and with hope, the cycle renews,
In the garden of life, we choose our views.
Seeds of intent, in abundance they thrive,
Creating a legacy, keeping dreams alive.

Unfolding Life's Patterns

Each day a layer, quietly unfurling,
Life's complex patterns, ever swirling.
Moments intertwine, a beautiful dance,
In the tapestry of time, we take our chance.

Ripples of laughter, whispers of grief,
In the fabric of life, we find belief.
Stitched with experiences, joys, and strife,
Unraveling secrets of this wondrous life.

With every heartbeat, a new thread spins,
Patterns emerge, where chaos begins.
Connected we are, with stories to share,
In the grand design, we're woven with care.

So let us embrace each woven line,
In the unfolding, our spirits entwine.
Life's patterns unique, a story to tell,
In the rich tapestry, we all dwell.

Melodies of the Committed

In the quiet moments we find our song,
Threads of purpose where we belong.
With each note sung, our spirits soar,
Together we rise, forever more.

With hands joined tightly, we face the storm,
In the heart of struggle, a bond is born.
Echoes of laughter that light the night,
A symphony built on shared delight.

The music whispers of dreams in flight,
Guiding us gently towards the light.
Each heartbeat counts, a rhythm divine,
In the dance of life, your hand in mine.

Through trials faced and battles won,
The melodies play, never to be done.
In shadows cast and in bright daylight,
Together we sing, our hearts unite.

Symphony of the Same

In a world where echoes intertwine,
The notes of sameness, a pleasing line.
With familiar chords that gently play,
A tune of comfort in the fray.

Each voice a thread in the woven sound,
Together in harmony, we are bound.
While every moment feels just like before,
It's in this sameness we find the core.

Through rituals danced in steady beat,
We find our rhythm, and the joy is sweet.
In the simple things, we come alive,
In the symphony of same, we thrive.

So let the music linger long,
In every heart, a treasured song.
Through days that mirror, we shall embrace,
The beauty found in our shared space.

The Pallet of Practice

With every stroke, the colors blend,
A canvas waiting, where dreams extend.
In practice found, we shape the hue,
Each moment crafted, a fresh debut.

Brushes dance in a gentle flow,
Layer by layer, our talents grow.
In patience learned, the masterpiece waits,
As time unfolds, we open the gates.

From deep blues of doubt to bright yellows of cheer,
Each color tells stories, both far and near.
With a steady hand, we paint our fate,
In the palette of life, it's never too late.

The art of practice, a journey we take,
In every mistake, new patterns we make.
So gather your colors, let heart be your guide,
In the palette of practice, let passion reside.

Constellations of Routine

Under the night sky, patterns appear,
Constellations bright, held so dear.
Each star a moment, a step in the dance,
In routines formed, we find our chance.

With habits crafted, our paths align,
In the rhythm of life, both yours and mine.
The whispers of dawn, the hush of dusk,
In daily motions, a trust we must.

Through cycles spinning, we learn and grow,
In the ordinary, the magic flows.
Each day a chapter, a line to weave,
In constellations of routine, we believe.

So gaze at the heavens, find comfort in fate,
In the patterns we form, it's never too late.
For every star shines, a story to tell,
In the constellations of routine, we dwell.

Milton Keynes UK
Ingram Content Group UK Ltd.
UKHW051811101024
449294UK00007BA/60